# RATIOS and PERCENTS

## MATH BUSTERS

Rebecca Wingard-Nelson

**E** **Enslow Publishers, Inc.**
40 Industrial Road
Box 398
Berkeley Heights, NJ 07922
USA

http://www.enslow.com

**Library of Congress Cataloging-in-Publication Data**

Wingard-Nelson, Rebecca.
Ratios and percents / Rebecca Wingard-Nelson.
      p. cm. — (Math busters)
    Summary: "A step-by-step guide to the basics of ratios and fractions"—Provided by publisher.
    Includes bibliographical references and index.
    ISBN-13: 978-0-7660-2878-4
    ISBN-10: 0-7660-2878-X
    1. Ratio and proportion—Juvenile literature. 2. Percentage—Juvenile literature. I. Title.
    QA117.W567 2008
  513.2'4—dc22

                                       2007012795

10 9 8 7 6 5 4 3 2 1

**To Our Readers:** We have done our best to make sure all Internet Addresses in this book were active and appropriate when we went to press. However, the author and the publisher have no control over and assume no liability for the material available on those Internet sites or on other Web sites they may link to. Any comments or suggestions can be sent by e-mail to comments@enslow.com or to the address on the back cover.

**Illustration credits:** © Artville/Artzooks, pp. 9, 14, 46; © Birch Design Studios/Artzooks, p. 39; © 2007 Jupiterimages Corporation, pp. 7, 11, 17, 18, 20, 23, 25, 27, 29, 31, 33, 37, 41, 43, 45, 48, 51, 53, 55, 57, 61.

**Cover photo:** © 2007 iStock International Inc.

Free Worksheets are available for this book at http://www.enslow.com. Search under the **Math Busters** series name. The publisher will provide access to the worksheets for five years from the book's first publication date.

# Contents

# Introduction

Not every person is an accountant,
engineer, rocket scientist, or math teacher.
However, every person does use math.

Most people never think, "I just used math to decide if I have
enough milk for this week!" But that is exactly what they did.
Math is everywhere; we just don't see it because it doesn't
always look like the math we do at school.

Math gives you the power to:
- determine the best route on a trip
- keep score in a game
- compare prices
- figure how much paint to buy
- plan a vacation schedule

Ratios and percents describe how amounts relate
to each other. You can compare the number of boys
to the number of girls in a class with a ratio.
A percent grade on a test compares the right answers
to all of the answers. Percents can also tell you how
much you can save by purchasing items on sale.

This book will help you understand ratios and percents.
It can be read from beginning to end,
or used to review a specific topic.

# ① Ratios

Ratios are a way to compare two numbers, quantities, or measurements.

## Reading and Writing Ratios

Ratios can be written in three ways.

1. Using the word "to":                   **3 to 2**
2. Using a colon:                          **3 : 2**
3. Using the fraction bar:                 **$\frac{3}{2}$**

No matter how you write a ratio, it is always read the same way,
**"three to two."**

The numbers in a ratio are called **terms.** In the ratio 3 : 2, 3 is the **first term**, and 2 is the **second term.**

## Parts and Wholes

*Jerry has 8 blue marbles and 4 green marbles. Marie has 7 red marbles and 4 green ones.*

*Write a ratio using the word "to" that compares Jerry's blue and green marbles.*

**Step 1:** Jerry has 8 blue marbles. This is the first term.     **8 to**

**Step 2:** Jerry has 4 green marbles. This is the second term.  **8 to 4**

**The ratio of Jerry's blue marbles to his green ones is 8 to 4.**
This ratio compares two parts (blue marbles and green marbles) of one whole thing (all of Jerry's marbles).

**Write a ratio using a colon (:) that compares Jerry's blue marbles to all of his marbles.**

**Step 1:** Jerry has 8 blue marbles. This is the first term.

8 :

**Step 2:** Jerry has a total of 12 marbles, 8 blue + 4 green. This is the second term.

8 : 12

**The ratio of Jerry's blue marbles to all of his marbles is 8 : 12.** This ratio compares one part (Jerry's blue marbles) to the whole thing (all of his marbles).

**Write a ratio using the fraction bar that compares Jerry's marbles to Marie's marbles.**

**Step 1:** Jerry has 12 marbles (8 blue and 4 green). This is the first term (the top number).

$\underline{12}$

**Step 2:** Marie has 11 marbles (7 red and 4 green). This is the second term (the bottom number).

$\dfrac{12}{11}$

**The ratio of Jerry's marbles to Marie's marbles is $\dfrac{12}{11}$.** This ratio compares one whole thing (Jerry's marbles) to another whole thing (Marie's marbles).

Ratios can look like fractions, but they are not always the same.

The denominator in a fraction always tells how many equal parts are in one whole.

$\dfrac{8 \text{ blue marbles}}{12 \text{ total marbles}}$     $\dfrac{8 \text{ blue marbles}}{4 \text{ green marbles}}$

Here $\dfrac{8}{12}$ is a ratio and a fraction.     Here $\dfrac{8}{4}$ is a ratio but not a fraction.

# ② Equivalent Ratios

Ratios that have the same
value are called equivalent ratios.
*Equivalent* means "equal to."

## Equivalent Ratios

Let's look at an example to help understand equivalent ratios.
Here is a pattern of dots.

There are 6 blue dots and 3 pink dots.
The ratio of blue to pink is **6 to 3.**

You can see that for every 2 blue dots there is 1 pink dot.
The ratio of each set of dots is **2 to 1.**

If you add one more set of dots, 2 blue and 1 pink, there are
8 blue dots and 4 pink dots. The ratio of blue to pink is **8 to 4.**

Each of these ratios, **6 to 3**, **2 to 1**, and **8 to 4**, describes the
same pattern. They are equal, or **equivalent ratios.**

# Finding Equivalent Ratios

*Jacinda can skate around the roller rink 15 times for every 10 times Moe can skate around. Write 2 ratios that are equivalent to 15 : 10.*

**Step 1:** You can rename ratios by multiplying both terms by the same number. Let's multiply both terms by 2.

$$15 : 10$$
$$15 \times 2 : 10 \times 2$$
$$30 : 20$$

**15 : 10 is equivalent to 30 : 20.**

**Step 2:** You can rename ratios by dividing both terms by the same number. Let's divide both terms by 5.

$$15 : 10$$
$$15 \div 5 : 10 \div 5$$
$$3 : 2$$

**15 : 10 is equivalent to 3 : 2.**

If you have 20 girls and 10 boys in a class, the ratio is 20 to 10. This can also be written as 2 to 1.

The ratio 2 to 1 tells you that for every two girls in the class, there is one boy. However, it does not tell you exactly how many girls and boys are in the class.

So, do not rewrite a ratio if you need to know the actual numbers.

# ③ Reducing Ratios

Knowing the factors of
numbers will help you reduce ratios.

## Factors

**factor**—A number that divides evenly into a given number.
The number 3 divides evenly into 12 (12 ÷ 3 = 4).
3 is a factor of 12.

**common factor**—A number that divides evenly into more
than one given number.
The factors of 12 are 1, 2, 3, 4, 6, and 12.
The factors of 6 are 1, 2, 3, and 6.
The common factors of 12 and 6 are  1, 2, 3, and 6.

**greatest common factor**—The largest number that divides
evenly into more than one given number.
The greatest common factor of 12 and 6 is 6.

## Reducing Ratios

*Reduce 24 : 6 to lower terms.*

**Step 1:** Reducing a ratio means writing it using smaller numbers.
To reduce a ratio, find a common factor of the terms.

The terms 24 and 6 are both divisible by 3,
so a common factor of 24 and 6 is 3.

**Step 2:** Divide both terms by
the common factor, 3.

$$24 : 6$$
$$24 ÷ 3 : 6 ÷ 3$$
$$8 : 2$$

**24 : 6 can be reduced to 8 : 2.**

# Lowest Terms

*Serena made 36 quesadillas and 12 salads. Write the ratio of quesadillas to salads in lowest terms.*

A ratio is in **lowest terms** when it cannot be reduced any more.

In lowest terms, the only common factor of the terms is 1.

**Step 1:** Write the ratio of quesadillas to salads. There are 36 quesadillas—this is the first term. There are 12 salads—this is the second term.

$$36 : 12$$

**Step 2:** Find the greatest common factor of 36 and 12.

List the factors of 36:     **1, 2, 3, 4, 6,** 9, **12,** 18, 36
List the factors of 12:     **1, 2, 3, 4, 6, 12**

The greatest common factor of 36 and 12 is 12.

**Step 3:** Divide both terms by the greatest common factor, 12.

$$36 : 12$$
$$36 \div 12 : 12 \div 12$$
$$3 : 1$$

**In lowest terms, the ratio of quesadillas to salads is 3 : 1.**

# ④ Rates

Rates are ratios that
compare two different kinds of
quantities, such as distance and time.

## Reading and Writing Rates

The types of quantities, called units, are included when you write a rate. Rates are usually written in two ways.

1. Using the word "per":  **35 students per 2 teachers**
2. Using the fraction bar:  $\dfrac{\textbf{35 students}}{\textbf{2 teachers}}$

Rates are read using the word "per" and the units.
**"Thirty-five students per two teachers"**

## Finding Rates

*A 2-pound package of cheese costs $6.00. Write a rate showing the price of cheese per number of pounds.*

**Step 1:** The rate is price per pounds, so the first term is the price. Write a dollar sign ($) to show the units are dollars.  **$6.00 per**

**Step 2:** The second term is pounds.  **$6.00 per 2 pounds**

**The cheese costs $6.00 per 2 pounds.**

# Reducing Rates

*A 2-pound package of cheese costs $6.00.*
*Write the rate in lowest terms.*

**Step 1:** Write the rate.                     **$6.00 per 2 pounds**

**Step 2:** Find the greatest common factor of 6 and 2.

List the factors of 6:        **1, 2**, 3, 6
List the factors of 2:        **1, 2**

The greatest common factor of 6 and 2 is 2.

**Step 3:** Divide both terms          **$6.00  per  2 pounds**
by the greatest common              **6.00 ÷ 2    2 ÷ 2**
factor, 2.                          **$3.00 per 1 pound**

**In lowest terms, the cheese costs $3.00 per pound.**

Rates are used every day.
Some even have their own names.

**Speed** compares how far you go to how
long it takes you (55 miles per hour).

**Mileage** compares how many miles you drive to
how much fuel you use (20 miles per gallon).

**Density** compares the amount of something to
the amount of space it takes up.
(10 seeds per square foot).

# ⑤ Ratios and Fractions

Ratios with fractions
are sometimes easier to use if they are
changed to ratios with whole numbers.

## Multiples

Multiples help you change fraction ratios to whole number ratios.

**multiple**—The product of a given number and any whole number is a multiple of that number.

**common multiples**—Numbers that are multiples of two or more given numbers.

**least common multiple**—The smallest common multiple, other than zero, of two or more given numbers.

## Fractions in Ratios

*When Omar practices his clarinet for $\frac{1}{4}$ hour, his mother lets him play video games for $\frac{1}{2}$ hour. Write a whole number ratio showing Omar's practice time to his game time.*

**Step 1:** Write the ratio of hours of practice time to hours of game time.

$$\frac{1}{4} \text{ to } \frac{1}{2}$$

**Step 2:** Find the least common multiple of the denominators.

List the multiples of 4:  **4, 8**, 12, 16, . . .
List the multiples of 2:  2, **4**, 6, **8**, . . .

**The least common multiple is 4.**

**Step 3:** Multiply each term by the least common multiple of the denominators.

$$\frac{1}{4} \times 4 \text{ to } \frac{1}{2} \times 4$$

To multiply fractions and whole numbers, change the whole numbers to fractions by writing them with a denominator of one.

$$\frac{1}{4} \times \frac{4}{1} \text{ to } \frac{1}{2} \times \frac{4}{1}$$

Reduce before you multiply by cancelling out common factors.
Cancel out 4s in the first term.
Cancel out 2s in the second term.

$$\frac{1}{\cancel{4}} \times \frac{\cancel{4}}{1} \text{ to } \frac{1}{\cancel{2}} \times \frac{\cancel{4}^{2}}{1}$$

Multiply the numerators.
Multiply the denominators.

$$\frac{1 \times 1}{1 \times 1} \text{ to } \frac{1 \times 2}{1 \times 1}$$

$$\frac{1}{1} \text{ to } \frac{2}{1}$$

**Step 4:** Reduce the ratio to lowest terms.        1 to 2

The ratio of Omar's practice time to his game time is 1 to 2.

# Mixed Numbers in Ratios

*Write the ratio $3\frac{1}{2}$ to 2 as a whole number ratio.*

**Step 1:** Write the original ratio.        $3\frac{1}{2}$ to 2

**Step 2:** Write mixed number terms as improper fractions.        $\frac{7}{2}$ to 2

**Step 3:** The second term is a whole number. When only one of the terms is a fraction, multiply each of the terms by the denominator of the fraction.
Multiply each term by 2.

$$\frac{7}{2} \times 2 \text{ to } 2 \times 2$$

$$\frac{7}{\cancel{2}} \times \frac{\cancel{2}}{1} \text{ to } 2 \times 2$$

$$\frac{7}{1} \text{ to } 4$$

**Step 4:** Reduce the ratio to lowest terms.        7 to 4

$3\frac{1}{2}$ **to 2 is the same as 7 to 4.**

# ⑥ Ratios and Decimals

Sometimes ratios contain decimals.
The decimals can be changed to whole
number ratios by moving the decimal points.

## Powers of Ten and Decimals

When a decimal is multiplied by a power of ten (like 10 or 100),
the decimal point moves to the right one place for each zero.

$$4.127 \times 10 = 41.27$$

$$4.127 \times 100 = 412.7$$

$$4.127 \times 1,000 = 4127$$

## Decimal Ratios

*Write the ratio 4 : 5.2 as a whole number ratio.*

| | |
|---|---|
| **Step 1:** There is one decimal place in 5.2. To move the decimal point one place right, you can multiply by 10. | $5.2 \times 10 = 52$ |
| **Step 2:** To find equivalent ratios, multiply both terms by the same number. Multiply both terms by 10. | $4 : 5.2$ <br> $4 \times 10 : 5.2 \times 10$ <br> $40 : 52$ |
| **Step 3:** Reduce the ratio to lowest terms. Divide 40 and 52 by their greatest common factor, 4. | $40 : 52$ <br> $40 \div 4 : 52 \div 4$ <br> $10 : 13$ |

**4 : 5.2 is the same as 10 : 13.**

# Move the Decimal Point

*A picture is 4.5 centimeters tall and 6.75 centimeters wide.*
*Write the ratio of height to width as a whole number ratio.*

**Step 1:** Write the original ratio.                    **4.5 to 6.75**

**Step 2:** Move the decimal point                    4.5 to 6.75
right the same number of places
in each term. Since 6.75 has two                    **450 to 675**
decimal places, move each decimal
point two places to the right.

**Step 3:** Reduce the ratio to lowest terms.         $\frac{450}{5}$ to $\frac{675}{5}$
When the greatest common factor is large, or
hard to find, you can reduce more than one time.      **90 to 135**
Divide 450 and 675 by 5 first.
Reduce again by dividing 90 and 135 by 5.              $\frac{90}{5}$ to $\frac{135}{5}$

                                                      **18 to 27**

Reduce again by dividing 18 and 27 by 9.              $\frac{18}{9}$ to $\frac{27}{9}$

                                                      **2 to 3**

**For this picture, the whole number
ratio of height to width is 2 to 3.**

Unit ratios and
unit rates always have one unit
in the second term.

## Unit Ratios and Rates

When the second term in a ratio is one unit (like one person or one hour), the ratio is called a **unit ratio.**
25 students to 1 teacher is a unit ratio.

When the second term in a rate is one unit, the rate is called a **unit rate.** $6 per 1 hour is a unit rate.

Unit rates usually do not include the 1 in the second term.
Instead of saying 50 miles per 1 hour, you say 50 miles per hour.

## Unit Ratios

*Sam mixed 5 parts of red paint and 2 parts of blue paint. How many times as much red paint did he use as blue paint?*

To solve this problem, find the unit ratio. A unit ratio tells you how many times larger or smaller the first term is than the second term.

**Step 1:** Write the original ratio of red paint to blue paint.

$$5 : 2$$

**Step 2:** To find a unit ratio, divide both terms by the second term.

$$5 \div 2 : 2 \div 2$$
$$2.5 : 1$$

**The ratio of red paint to blue paint is 2.5 to 1. This means Sam used 2.5 times as much red paint as he did blue paint.**

# Unit Rates

*A painter earns $600.00 per 40-hour week.*
*How much does the painter earn per hour?*

To solve this problem, find the unit rate, or rate per one hour.

| | |
|---|---|
| **Step 1:** Write the original rate. | **$600.00 per 40 hours** |

| | |
|---|---|
| **Step 2:** Divide both terms by the second term, 40. | $\frac{\$600.00}{40}$ **per** $\frac{40}{40}$ **hours** |
| | **$15.00 per hour** |

**The painter earns $15.00 per hour.**

*Darlene used 4 gallons of fuel to drive 70 miles.*
*What was her fuel mileage?*

To solve this problem, find the unit rate. Fuel mileage is the unit rate for the number of miles driven per gallon of fuel.

Problems that ask you to find the mileage, speed, or any other common rate are asking for the unit rate.

| | |
|---|---|
| **Step 1:** Write the original rate. | **70 miles per 4 gallons** |

| | |
|---|---|
| **Step 2:** Divide both terms by the second term, 4. | $\frac{70}{4}$ **miles per** $\frac{4}{4}$ **gallons** |
| | $17\frac{1}{2}$ **miles per gallon** |

**Darlene's fuel mileage was $17\frac{1}{2}$ miles per gallon.**

Unit ratios can be written using decimals or fractions in the first term.

$17\frac{1}{2}$ miles per hour

or

17.5 miles per hour

Unit prices let you compare
prices when items are sold in different sizes.

## Unit Prices

The **price** of an item is usually the total price for a can, bottle, box, or container of something. For example, the price of a 6-ounce can of juice might be $0.78.

**Unit price** is the price of one measurement unit, like a pound, an ounce, a quart, or any other weight or volume unit. The unit price for the can of juice is $0.13 per ounce ($0.78 ÷ 6 ounces = $0.13 per ounce).

## The Better Buy

*A 9-ounce bottle of water costs $0.99. A 20-ounce bottle of water costs $1.60. Which is the better buy?*

To solve this problem, compare the unit prices.

**Step 1:** Write a rate for each bottle that shows the cost per number of units. The units in this problem are ounces of water.

$0.99 per 9 ounces          $1.60 per 20 ounces

**Step 2:** Find the unit rate for each package by dividing each by its second term.

$$\frac{\$0.99}{9} \text{ per } \frac{9}{9} \text{ ounces} \qquad \frac{\$1.60}{20} \text{ per } \frac{20}{20} \text{ ounces}$$

$0.11 per ounce          $0.08 per ounce

**Step 3:** Compare.        $0.08 is less than $0.11

**The 20-ounce bottle of water is the better buy because each ounce of water costs $0.08.**

*One package of 8 hotdog buns costs $1.20. A package*
*of 12 buns costs $1.68. Which package is the better buy?*

**Step 1:** Write a rate for each package that shows the cost per number of units. The units in this problem are hotdog buns.

$1.20 per 8 buns          $1.68 per 12 buns

**Step 2:** Find the unit rate for each package by dividing each by its second term.

$$\frac{\$1.20}{8} \text{ per } \frac{8}{8} \text{ buns} \qquad \frac{\$1.68}{12} \text{ per } \frac{12}{12} \text{ buns}$$

$0.15 per bun          $0.14 per bun

**Step 3:** Compare.

**$0.15 is more than $0.14.**

**The package with 12 buns is the better buy.**

## Other Rates

*Clara typed 128 words in 4 minutes. Zachary typed 165 words in 5 minutes. Who typed faster?*

You can compare any kind of rates by finding the unit rates first.

Unit price is only part of smart shopping.

If you only have 8 hotdogs, you will not use 12 buns. The smaller package is the better buy because it costs less, and you won't waste any buns.

If you don't like the taste of one kind of bun, it may be worth spending more for the kind you like.

**Step 1:** Write the original typing rate for each person.

| Clara | Zachary |
|-------|---------|
| 128 words per 4 minutes | 165 words per 5 minutes |

**Step 2:** Find the unit rate each person typed.

$$\frac{128}{4} \text{ words per } \frac{4}{4} \text{ minutes} \qquad \frac{165}{5} \text{ words per } \frac{5}{5} \text{ minutes}$$

32 words per minute          33 words per minute

**Step 3:** Compare.          **32 words per minute is less than 33 words per minute.**

**Zachary typed faster than Clara.**

# ⑨ Distance, Rate, and Time

Speed is a rate that tells
how fast you do something.
Speed compares how much you do or how far you
go to the amount of time it takes.

## Speed

*Harold drove 234 miles in 4.5 hours.*
*What was his average speed?*

| | |
|---|---|
| **Step 1:** Write the original rate. | **234 miles per 4.5 hours** |
| **Step 2:** Divide both terms by the second term, 4.5. | $\frac{234}{4.5}$ **miles per** $\frac{4.5}{4.5}$ **hours** |
| | **52 miles per hour** |

**Harold's average speed
was 52 miles per hour.**

## The Distance Formula

A **formula** is an equation that uses words or symbols
to show a relationship that is always true.

The relationship between distance, rate, and time is so important
that it has its own formula.

The distance formula is **distance = rate × time.**

You can always find how far something goes (distance)
by multiplying how fast it moves (a unit rate) by how much time
it takes (time).

# The Distance Formula

*You are walking at a rate of 3 mph (miles per hour). If you walk for 2 hours, how many miles will you have walked?*

**Step 1:** The distance formula tells you that if you multiply a unit rate (3 mph) by a time (2 hours), you can find the distance traveled. Multiply 3 miles per hour by 2 hours.

$$3 \times 2 = 6$$

**You will have walked 6 miles.**

The units used in a problem must match.

If the speed is in miles per **hour**, you can't use **minutes** for the time. Change the time to hours first.

If the speed uses kilometers, the distance is in **kilometers**, not **miles**.

*Gina rode an ATV for $\frac{1}{2}$ hour at a steady rate of 60 km per hour. How many kilometers did she ride?*

**Step 1:** Multiply the unit rate (60 km per hour) by the time ($\frac{1}{2}$ hour).

$$60 \times \frac{1}{2} = 30$$

**Gina rode 30 kilometers.**

# ⑩ Proportions

Proportions are used to
show that two ratios are equal.

## Proportions

A **proportion** is an equation that shows equivalent ratios. Proportions are usually written using fraction bars.

$$\frac{2}{3} = \frac{4}{6}$$

Proportions can also be written using colons.

$$2 : 3 = 4 : 6$$

No matter how you write a proportion, it can always be read the same way.

**"Two is to three as four is to six."**

Proportions have **four** terms.

$$\frac{\textbf{first term}}{\textbf{second term}} = \frac{\textbf{third term}}{\textbf{fourth term}}$$

## Proportional

*Are the ratios $\frac{2}{6}$ and $\frac{6}{18}$ proportional?*

**Step 1:** Write the two ratios as a proportion.

$$\frac{2}{6} = \frac{6}{18}$$

**Step 2:** Reduce each ratio to lowest terms. The proportion is **true** because the ratios are equivalent. If the ratios were not equivalent, you would say the proportion is **NOT true**.

$$\frac{2 \div 2}{6 \div 2} = \frac{6 \div 6}{18 \div 6}$$

$$\frac{1}{3} = \frac{1}{3}$$

**Yes, the ratios $\frac{2}{6}$ and $\frac{6}{18}$ are proportional.**

# Cross Multiplication

**Cross multiplication** means to multiply diagonally. Multiply the first term by the fourth term and multiply the second term by the third term. The answers, called **cross products**, are the same in a true proportion. If the answers are not the same, the proportion is not true.

$$\frac{1}{4} \times \frac{2}{8} \qquad \begin{array}{l} 4 \times 2 = 8 \\ 1 \times 8 = 8 \end{array} \bigg> 8 = 8$$

Cross multiplication is written as:

**first term × fourth term = second term × third term**

$$1 \times 8 = 4 \times 2$$

# Cross Products

*A picture is 3 inches tall and 2 inches wide. Jerry used his computer to change the size of the picture to 4 inches tall and 6 inches wide. Are the pictures proportional?*

**Step 1:** Write the ratio of height to width for each picture.

| original | new |
|---|---|
| $\dfrac{3 \text{ in}}{2 \text{ in}}$ | $\dfrac{4 \text{ in}}{6 \text{ in}}$ |

**Step 2:** Cross multiply. If the cross products are equal, the ratios are proportional. The cross products are NOT equal, so the proportion is NOT true.

$$\frac{3}{2} \overset{?}{\underset{?}{=}} \frac{4}{6}$$

$$3 \times 6 = 2 \times 4$$

$$18 \neq 8$$

**The pictures are not proportional.**

# ⑪ Solving Proportions

You can use what
you know about proportions
to find an unknown term.

## Simple Proportions

*The ratio of boys to girls in Megan's class is 2 to 3.*
*If there are 12 boys in the class, how many girls are there?*

**Step 1:** You can find the number of girls
in the class by setting up a proportion.
The ratio given is boys to girls, so the
ratio on the other side of the proportion
should also be boys to girls. Fill in the ratios
with the numbers given in the problem.

$$\frac{\text{boys}}{\text{girls}} = \frac{\text{boys}}{\text{girls}}$$

$$\frac{2}{3} = \frac{12}{?}$$

**Step 2:** You can solve a proportion
by finding equivalent ratios using mental
math. To change the first term (2) to 12, you
multiply by 6. Do the same to the second term (3).
$3 \times 6 = 18$.

$$\frac{2}{3} = \frac{12}{18}$$

**There are 18 girls in Megan's class.**

Remember:
To find equivalent ratios,
multiply or divide both terms
by the same number.

# Cross Products

*Inez uses 2 cups of flour to make 12 biscuits. How many cups of flour does she need to make 18 biscuits?*

**Step 1:** Set up a proportion.

flour ⟶ $\dfrac{2}{12} = \dfrac{?}{18}$ ⟵ biscuits

**Step 2:** In proportions, the cross products are equal. Show the cross multiplication. Multiply 2 × 18.

$2 \times 18 = 12 \times ?$
$36 = 12 \times ?$

**Step 3:** You need to find the number that when multiplied by 12 equals 36. Divide 36 by 12.

The solved proportion is $\dfrac{2}{12} = \dfrac{3}{18}$

$36 = 12 \times ?$
$36 \div 12 = 3$

**Inez needs 3 cups of flour to make 18 biscuits.**

# Proportions Shortcut

*Inez uses 2 cups of flour to make 12 biscuits. How many biscuits can she make using 1 cup of flour?*

**Step 1:** Set up a proportion.

flour ⟶ $\dfrac{2}{12} = \dfrac{1}{?}$ ⟵ biscuits

**Step 2:** Cross multiply only the two terms that are given. These give you a cross product of 12.

$\dfrac{2}{12} \diagup\!\!\!\!\diagup \dfrac{1}{?}$

$12 \times 1 = 12$

**Step 3:** Divide this cross product (12) by the known term that is left (2). The result is the unknown term.

The solved proportion is $\dfrac{2}{12} = \dfrac{1}{6}$

$\dfrac{2}{12} \diagup\!\!\!\!\diagup \dfrac{1}{?} \; 12$

$12 \div 2 = 6$

**Inez can make 6 biscuits with 1 cup of flour.**

# ⑫ Ratios in Geometry

Anything related to
the shape or size of something is
also related to geometry.

## Similar Shapes

*In geometry, similar shapes have
measurements that are in proportion.
They have the same ratio.
These two rectangles are similar.
How tall is the blue rectangle?*

4 cm

5 cm

6 cm

?

**Step 1:** Set up a proportion relating
the height and width of each rectangle.
Write in the measurements you know
from the rectangles.

$$\frac{\text{height}}{\text{width}} = \frac{\text{height}}{\text{width}}$$

$$\frac{5 \text{ cm}}{4 \text{ cm}} = \frac{?}{6 \text{ cm}}$$

**Step 2:** Cross multiply the terms
that are both known, 5 and 6.

$$\frac{5 \text{ cm}}{4 \text{ cm}} \searrow \frac{?}{6 \text{ cm}}$$

$$5 \times 6 = 30$$

**Step 3:** Divide by the term that is left, 4.
The solved proportion is $\frac{5}{4} = \frac{7.5}{6}$

$$30 \div 4 = 7.5$$

**The blue rectangle is 7.5 cm tall.**

The word **geometry**
comes from the Greek
root words
*geo*, meaning earth, and
*metron*, meaning measure.

# Shadow Problems

*Alex is standing beside a statue. Alex is 54 inches tall. His shadow is 9 inches long. The shadow of the statue is 21 inches long. How tall is the statue?*

**Step 1:** Heights of objects and the lengths of their shadows are proportional when they are measured at the same time of day. Set up a proportion using the measurements in the problem.

$$\frac{\text{Alex} \atop \text{height}}{\text{shadow length}} = \frac{\text{Statue} \atop \text{height}}{\text{shadow length}}$$

$$\frac{54 \text{ in}}{9 \text{ in}} = \frac{?}{21 \text{ in}}$$

**Step 2:** You can reduce the ratio that you know to make cross multiplication easier.

$$\frac{54 \text{ in} \div 9}{9 \text{ in} \div 9} \text{ becomes } \frac{6 \text{ in}}{1 \text{ in}}$$

**Step 3:** Write the proportion using the reduced ratio.

$$\frac{6 \text{ in}}{1 \text{ in}} = \frac{?}{21 \text{ in}}$$

**Step 4:** Cross multiply the terms that are both known, 6 and 21.

$$6 \times 21 = 126$$

**Step 5:** Divide by the term that is left, 1.

$$126 \div 1 = 126$$

The solved proportion is

$$\frac{54 \text{ inches}}{9 \text{ inches}} = \frac{126 \text{ inches}}{21 \text{ inches}}$$

**The statue is 126 inches tall.**

Check the answer to the shadow problem by reducing each ratio to lowest terms.

$$\frac{54 \div 9}{9 \div 9} = \frac{126 \div 21}{21 \div 21}$$

$$\frac{6}{1} = \frac{6}{1}$$

The proportion is true.

# 13 Scale Drawings and Models

Scale drawings and models
are used to show big or small objects
in a manageable size.

## Scale

A **scale** is a ratio that compares the measurements of a drawing
or model to the measurements of the object it represents.
The model or drawing measurement is always the first term.
The real object measurement is the second term

Scales are written like other ratios. The scale **1 inch to 2 feet**
means if an object is 2 feet tall, the drawing will be 1 inch tall.
Sometimes a scale is written using the = sign, **1 inch = 2 feet**.

There are two kinds of scale drawings and models.
A **reduction** makes a model that is smaller than the object.
An **enlargement** makes a model that is larger than the object.

## Reduction

*Jennifer is making a map of her town. The map scale is 1 inch to
2 miles. Jennifer's house is exactly 4 miles from the school.
On her map, how far should her house be from the school?*

**Step 1:** Maps are reductions. The scale tells you that on the map,
1 inch is the same as 2 miles in real distance.

Set up a proportion. Use the scale as the first ratio.
Fill in the part of the second ratio that you know.

scale inches $\longrightarrow$
real miles $\longrightarrow$ $\dfrac{1}{2} = \dfrac{?}{4}$

**Step 2:** This is a simple proportion. Solve it by finding equivalent ratios. To change the second term (2) to 4, you multiply by 2. Do the same to the first term (1). $1 \times 2 = 2$.

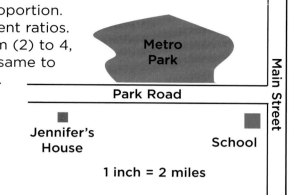

$$\frac{1 \, (\times \, 2)}{2 \, (\times \, 2)} = \frac{2}{4}$$

**On the map, Jennifer's house should be 2 inches from the school.**

# Enlargement

*A model of a ladybug is made at a scale of 1 meter = 0.5 cm. The model is 0.8 meters long. How many centimeters long is the real ladybug?*

**Step 1:** Remember, the scaled measurement is the first term, and the real life measurement is the second term. The scale tells you that for every 1 meter of the model, the ladybug measures 0.5 cm. Since the model is larger than the real ladybug, this is an enlargement.

Set up a proportion. Use the scale as the first ratio. Fill in the part of the second ratio that you know.

$$\text{scale meters} \longrightarrow \frac{1}{0.5} = \frac{0.8}{?} \longleftarrow \text{real centimeters}$$

**Step 2:** Cross multiply the terms that are both known, 0.5 and 0.8.          $0.5 \times 0.8 = 0.4$

**Step 3:** Divide by the term that is left, 1.          $0.4 \div 1 = 0.4$

$$\text{scale meters} \longrightarrow \frac{1}{0.5} = \frac{0.8}{0.4} \longleftarrow \text{real centimeters}$$

**The real ladybug is 0.4 centimeters long.**

# ⑭ The Golden Ratio

One ratio is seen repeating itself in art, biology, nature, architecture and mathematics. It is called the golden ratio.

## The Golden Ratio

The golden ratio is a special ratio that is about **1 : 1.62**.

The modern idea of the golden ratio was discovered, but not invented, by a man named **Leonardo Fibonacci**.
The ancient Egyptians, Mayans, and Greeks used the golden ratio in their art and architecture.

## The Golden Rectangle

*A golden rectangle looks nice. Its length and width are in a ratio that is close to the golden ratio. A computer screen is 15 inches tall. Find the width if the screen is a golden rectangle.*

**Step 1:** Set up a proportion using the golden ratio as the first term. The height (length) of a computer screen is smaller than the width. Write the length as the corresponding term to the smaller term, 1. The length to width ratio is 1 to 1.62. Fill in the part of the second ratio that you know.

$$\text{length} \longrightarrow \frac{1}{1.62} = \frac{15 \text{ in}}{?} \longleftarrow \text{width}$$

**Step 2:** Cross multiply the terms that are both known, 1.62 and 15.

$$1.62 \times 15 = 24.3$$

**Step 3:** Divide by the term that is left, 1.

$$24.3 \div 1 = 24.3$$

$$\text{length} \longrightarrow \frac{1}{1.62} = \frac{15 \text{ in}}{24.3 \text{ in}} \longleftarrow \text{width}$$

**The screen is 24.3 inches wide.**

# The Golden Ratio in Your Body

*An average adult hand is about 18 cm long from the tip of the middle finger to the wrist. The length of an average adult forearm (wrist to elbow) is about 29 cm. Is the ratio of hand length to forearm length the golden ratio?*

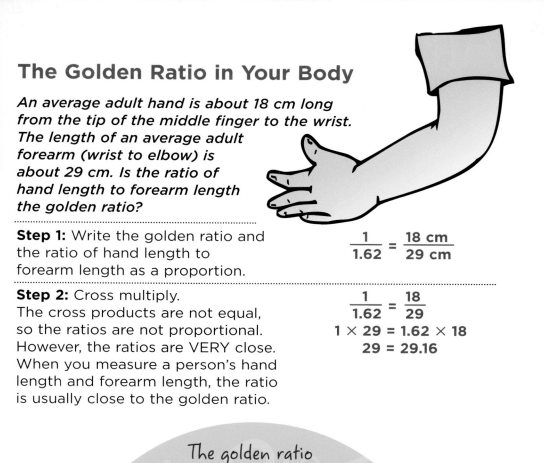

**Step 1:** Write the golden ratio and the ratio of hand length to forearm length as a proportion.

$$\frac{1}{1.62} = \frac{18 \text{ cm}}{29 \text{ cm}}$$

**Step 2:** Cross multiply. The cross products are not equal, so the ratios are not proportional. However, the ratios are VERY close. When you measure a person's hand length and forearm length, the ratio is usually close to the golden ratio.

$$\frac{1}{1.62} = \frac{18}{29}$$
$$1 \times 29 = 1.62 \times 18$$
$$29 = 29.16$$

The golden ratio can also be found in other parts of your body.

Try comparing the length of the segments in your fingers.

Try the length from your foot to your belly button and from your foot to the top of your head.

Remember, everyone is different, so the ratios will not be exactly the same. But they will be close. And they will be close to the golden ratio.

# Alternate Proportions

A proportion
can be written another way
and still be true.

## Corresponding Terms

There are two ratios and four terms in a proportion.
Terms that are in the same place in each ratio are called
**corresponding terms.**

$$\frac{\text{first}}{\text{second}} = \frac{\text{third}}{\text{fourth}}$$

The **first** and **third** term are corresponding terms.
The **second** and **fourth** term are corresponding terms.

## Find Corresponding Terms

*What are the corresponding terms in the proportion 1 : 3 = 5 : 15?*

**Step 1:** Corresponding terms are in the
same place in each ratio.
1 is the first term in the first ratio.
5 is the first term in the second ratio.

**1 and 5 are corresponding terms.**

$$1 : 3 = 5 : 15$$
or
$$\frac{1}{3} = \frac{5}{15}$$

3 is the second term in the first ratio.
15 is the second term in the second ratio.

**3 and 15 are corresponding terms.**

$$1 : 3 = 5 : 15$$
or
$$\frac{1}{3} = \frac{5}{15}$$

# Alternate Proportion

Corresponding terms in a true proportion are also in proportion. The proportion made by corresponding terms is called the **alternate proportion.**

$$\frac{1}{2} = \frac{3}{6}$$

can be written as

$$\frac{1}{3} = \frac{2}{6}$$

# Alternate Proportions

*The proportion 3 : 25 = 12 : 100 is true. Write the alternate proportion, and check to make sure it is true.*

**Step 1:** Write the original proportion using fraction bars. This makes it easier to find the corresponding terms.

$$\frac{3}{25} = \frac{12}{100}$$

**Step 2:** The first set of corresponding terms is 3 and 12. Write 3 and 12 as the first ratio in the alternate proportion.

$$\frac{3}{25} = \frac{12}{100} \qquad \frac{3}{12} = \underline{\quad}$$

**Step 3:** The second set of corresponding terms is 25 and 100. Write 25 and 100 as the second ratio.

$$\frac{3}{25} = \frac{12}{100} \qquad \frac{3}{25} = \frac{25}{100}$$

The alternate proportion is $\frac{3}{12} = \frac{25}{100}$ .

**Step 4:** Check the alternate proportion. Reduce each ratio to lowest terms.

$$\frac{3 \div 3}{12 \div 3} = \frac{25 \div 25}{100 \div 25}$$

$$\frac{1}{4} = \frac{1}{4}$$

The reduced ratios are the same, so the alternate proportion is true.

You can also check to see if a proportion is true by seeing if the cross products are equal.

# ⑯ Percents and Ratios

Percents are ratios that have
100 as the second term.
The word *percent* means *per hundred*.

## Percents

Percents are written using the percent sign, **%**.

25% is read as twenty-five percent.
25% means 25 per 100, or 25 : 100.

| | |
|---|---|
| Percents can be less than 100. | 42% or 42 : 100 |
| Percents can be equal to 100. | 100% or 100 : 100 |
| Percents can be greater than 100. | 150% or 150 : 100 |

## Modeling Percents

*Use a model to show 35%.*

**Step 1:** One way to model percents is to use a grid with 100 squares. 35% means 35 per hundred, so color 35 of the 100 squares.

**35% of the grid is colored.**

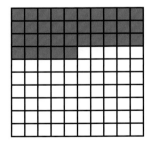

*Use a model to show 100%.*

**Step 1:** 100% means 100 per hundred, so color 100 of the 100 squares.

**100% of the grid is colored.**

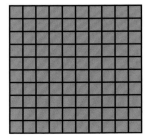

# Writing a Ratio as a Percent

*On Ray's mp3 player, the ratio of jazz music to all of his music is 78 to 100. What percent of the music is jazz?*

**Step 1:** Write the ratio of jazz music to all music.          **78 : 100**

**Step 2:** When the second term is 100, you can replace the term with the percent symbol, %.          **78%**

To write a fraction or ratio as a percent when the second term is not 100, see pages 39 and 46.

**78% of the music on Ray's mp3 player is jazz.**

# Writing a Percent as a Ratio

*Write 48% as a ratio.*

**Step 1:** The first term of the ratio is the number part of the percent, 48.          **48 :**

**Step 2:** The second term is always 100.          **48 : 100**

**Step 3:** Reduce the ratio to lowest terms. Divide both terms by their greatest common factor, 4.          **48 ÷ 4 : 100 ÷ 4**
**12 : 25**

**48% as a ratio is 12 : 25.**

*Write 150% as a ratio.*

**Step 1:** The first term of the ratio is the number part of the percent, 150.          **150 :**

**Step 2:** The second term is always 100.          **150 : 100**

**Step 3:** Reduce the ratio to lowest terms. Divide both terms by their greatest common factor, 50.          **150 ÷ 50 : 100 ÷ 50**
**3 : 2**

**150% as a ratio is 3 : 2.**

# Percents, Fractions, and Decimals

**(17)**

Percents can be written as
fractions and decimals.

## Rewriting Percents

| **As fractions:** | | **89%** | **151%** |
|---|---|---|---|
| A percent is written as a fraction | | $\frac{89}{100}$ | $\frac{151}{100}$ |
| with a denominator of 100. | | | |
| The percentage, or number part | | | |
| of the percent, is the numerator. | | | |

| **As decimals:** | | **89%** | **151%** |
|---|---|---|---|
| A percent is written as a decimal | | 0.89 | 1.51 |
| by dropping the percent sign and | | | |
| moving the decimal point two places left. | | | |

## Rewriting a Percent

*Write 35% as a fraction and a decimal.*

**Step 1:** Write 35% as a fraction. Write the number part, 35, in the numerator. Write 100 in the denominator.

$$\frac{35}{100}$$

Reduce the fraction to lowest terms by dividing the numerator and denominator by their greatest common factor, 5.

$$\frac{35 \div 5}{100 \div 5} = \frac{7}{20}$$

**Step 2:** Write 35% as a decimal.
Drop the percent sign.
In a whole number, like 35, the decimal point is on the right of the ones digit.
Move the decimal point two places left.

35%
35.
0.35

$$35\% = \frac{35}{100} = 0.35$$

# Decimals as Percents

*Write 0.23, 0.6, and 1.27 as percents.*

| | 0.23 | 0.6 | 1.27 |
|---|---|---|---|
| **Step 1:** Multiply each decimal by 100%. When you multiply by 100, the decimal point moves 2 places to the right. | 23 | 60 | 127 |
| **Step 2:** Write the percent signs. | 23% | 60% | 127% |

**0.23 = 23%, 0.6 = 60%, and 1.27 = 127%.**

# Fractions as Percents

*In Bob's office, $\frac{1}{20}$ of the employees have beards. What percent of the employees have beards?*

**Step 1:** Multiply the fraction by 100.

$$\frac{1}{20} \times 100 = \frac{1}{20} \times \frac{100}{1} = \frac{100}{20}$$

**Step 2:** Reduce the fraction to lowest terms.

$$\frac{100}{20} = 5$$

**Step 3:** Write the percent sign.    5%

**5% of the employees have beards.**

You can also write a fraction as a percent by writing it as a decimal first.

1. Write the fraction as a decimal by dividing the numerator by the denominator.

2. Write the decimal as a percent.

39

Percents and Proportions

Proportions can be used
to solve percent problems.
Just use the percent as one of the ratios.

## Proportions in Percent Problems

Percent problems relate a percent, a part, and a whole.
You can solve percent problems by writing the percent as a
ratio and setting up a proportion.

$$\frac{\text{percentage}}{100} = \frac{\text{part}}{\text{whole}}$$

## Using Proportions

*Dr. Price saw 20 patients on Monday. Of those patients, 60%
had cavities. How many of the patients on Monday had cavities?*

**Step 1:** Set up a proportion.
Write 60% as a ratio.

$$\frac{60}{100} = \underline{\hspace{2cm}}$$

**Step 2:** The second ratio compares
the patients with cavities to all of
the patients. You know there were
a total of 20 patients on Monday.
You are trying to find how many of
them had cavities.

$$\frac{60}{100} = \frac{\text{part}}{\text{whole}}$$

$$\frac{60}{100} = \frac{?}{20}$$

**Step 3:** Solve the proportion.
Cross multiply the terms you know.
Divide by the term that is left.
The solved proportion is $\frac{60}{100} = \frac{12}{20}$

$$60 \times 20 = 1{,}200$$
$$1{,}200 \div 100 = 12$$

**12 of the patients on Monday had cavities.**

# Percents and Money

*A $3.00 tube of toothpaste is marked 40% off this week. How much will you save if you buy toothpaste this week?*

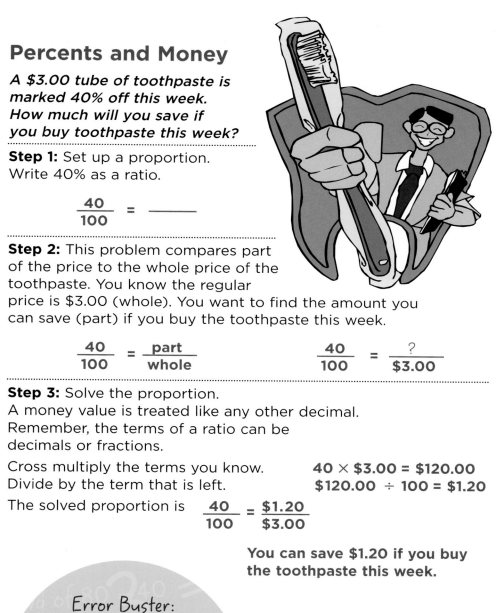

**Step 1:** Set up a proportion. Write 40% as a ratio.

$$\frac{40}{100} = \underline{\qquad}$$

**Step 2:** This problem compares part of the price to the whole price of the toothpaste. You know the regular price is $3.00 (whole). You want to find the amount you can save (part) if you buy the toothpaste this week.

$$\frac{40}{100} = \frac{part}{whole} \qquad\qquad \frac{40}{100} = \frac{?}{\$3.00}$$

**Step 3:** Solve the proportion. A money value is treated like any other decimal. Remember, the terms of a ratio can be decimals or fractions.

Cross multiply the terms you know.  40 × $3.00 = $120.00
Divide by the term that is left.  $120.00 ÷ 100 = $1.20

The solved proportion is  $\dfrac{40}{100} = \dfrac{\$1.20}{\$3.00}$

**You can save $1.20 if you buy the toothpaste this week.**

*Error Buster: Always include the decimal point and dollar sign in the answer when you solve a money problem.*

You can use a
multiplication statement to
find the percent of a number.

## The Percent Equation

Remember, percent problems relate three numbers: a whole,
a percent, and a part. This statement relates the numbers
to each other.

**Percent of whole is part.**
**50% of 20 is 10.**

You can change this statement to an equation.
"Of" means multiplication and "is" means equals.

**percent × whole = part**
**50% × 20 = 10**

## Finding the Percent of a Number

*What is 25% of 60?*

**Step 1:** Write the percent equation.   **percent × whole = part**
Put in the numbers that you know.   **25% × 60 = ___**

**Step 2:** Write the percent as a decimal.
**0.25 × 60 = ___**

**Step 3:** Multiply.   **0.25 × 60 = 15**

**25% of 60 is 15.**

You can write
the percent as a
decimal or a fraction.
25% is 1/4.
1/4 × 60 = 15.

# Word Problem Percents

*Marci wants to put 15% of her paycheck in a savings account.*
*If her paycheck is $200.00, how much should she put in savings?*

To solve this problem, find 15% of $200.00.

**Step 1:** Write the percent equation.
Put in the numbers you know.

$$\text{percent} \times \text{whole} = \text{part}$$
$$15\% \times 200.00 = \_\_\_$$

**Step 2:** Write the percent as a decimal.

$$0.15 \times 200.00 = \_\_\_$$

**Step 3:** Multiply.

$$0.15 \times 200.00 = 30.00$$
$$15\% \text{ of } 200.00 \text{ is } 30.00$$

**Marci should put $30.00 in a savings account.**

# Fractions in Percents

*What is $\frac{1}{3}\%$ of 1,200?*

**Step 1:** Write the percent equation.
Put in the numbers you know.

$$\text{percent} \times \text{whole} = \text{part}$$
$$\frac{1}{3}\% \times 1{,}200 = \_\_\_$$

**Step 2:** Write the percent as a fraction.
Percents are written as fractions by
dividing the percent by 100.

$$\frac{1}{3}\% = \frac{1}{3} \div 100$$

To divide fractions, multiply the first
number by the reciprocal of the second.

$$\frac{1}{3} \div 100 = \frac{1}{3} \times \frac{1}{100}$$
$$= \frac{1}{300}$$

**Step 3:** Put the fraction into the
percent equation, then multiply.
When multiplying fractions,
you can cancel out like factors
before you multiply.

$\frac{1}{3}\%$ of 1,200 is 4.

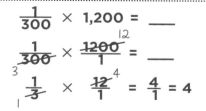

43

In most problems,
the part is less than the whole.
Some problems have a part that is
equal to or greater than the whole.

## 100%

*D'Jon set a goal to sell 72 used cars last year.*
*He sold 100% of his goal. How many used cars did D'Jon sell?*

To solve this problem, find 100% of 72.

| | **percent × whole = part** |
|---|---|
| **Step 1:** Write the percent equation. Put in the numbers you know. | **100% × 72 = ___** |
| **Step 2:** Write the percent as a decimal. | **1.00 × 72 = ___** |
| **Step 3:** Multiply. | **1.00 × 72 = 72** |

When the percent is 100%,
the part is always equal
to the whole.

**100% of 72 is 72.**

**D'Jon sold 72 used cars last year.**

Think about it:

100% as a fraction is $\frac{100}{100}$, or 1.

100% as a decimal is 1.00, or 1.

What do you get when you multiply one by a number?

The same number!

# Percents Larger Than 100%

*Phillip needs new jeans. The price of a pair of jeans today is 130% of what is was last month. If the jeans cost $27.00 last month, how much do they cost today? What is the difference in price?*

**Step 1:** Write the percent equation. Put in the numbers you know.

percent × whole = part
130% × $27.00 = ___

**Step 2:** Write the percent as a decimal.  1.30 × $27.00 = ___

**Step 3:** Multiply.  1.30 × $27.00 = $35.10

**Today, the jeans cost $35.10**

**Step 4:** Find the difference in price. Subtract the cost last month from the cost today.

$35.10
− $27.00
$ 8.10

**The jeans cost $8.10 more today.**

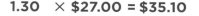

# Use a Proportion

*What is 150% of 200?*

**Step 1:** Set up a proportion. Write 150% as a ratio.

$$\frac{150}{100} = \frac{part}{whole}$$

**Step 2:** You can use the percent statement to decide which number is the part, and which is the whole.

Percent statement:  percent of whole is part
Problem statement: 150% of 200 is ____
200 is the whole. Write it in the proportion.

$$\frac{150}{100} = \frac{part}{200}$$

When the percent is over 100%, the part is greater than the whole.

300 > 200

**Step 3:** Solve the proportion. Cross multiply the terms you know.

**150 × 200 = 30,000**

Divide by the term that remains.

**30,000 ÷ 100 = 300**

The solved proportion is

$$\frac{150}{100} = \frac{300}{200}$$

**150% of 200 is 300.**

45

# ㉑ Relating Numbers by Percents

You can find what percent
one number is of another by using what
you already know about percents.

## First Write a Ratio

*There are 40 students in the marching band. Of those students, 7 play trombones. What percent of the marching band students play trombones?*

**Step 1:** Write the ratio of students who play trombones to the total number of students in the marching band.

$$\frac{\text{trombones}}{\text{total band}} \qquad \frac{7}{40}$$

**Step 2:** Write the ratio as a decimal by dividing the first term by the second term.

$$\frac{7}{40} = 7 \div 40$$

$$\frac{7}{40} = 0.175$$

```
      0.175
  40)7.000
   - 40
     300
   - 280
     200
   -  200
       0
```

**Step 3:** Write 0.175 as a percent. Move the decimal point 2 places right. Write the percent symbol.

$$0.175 = 17.5\%$$

**17.5% of the marching band students play trombones.**

46

# Use a Proportion

*What percent of 48 is 30?*

**Step 1:** Set up a proportion. Remember, a percent is a ratio with a second term of 100.

$$\frac{\text{percentage}}{100} = \frac{\text{part}}{\text{whole}}$$

**Step 2:** Fill in what you know.

$$\frac{\text{percentage}}{100} = \frac{30}{48}$$

> Percent Buster:
> Use the percent statement to decide which number is the part, and which is the whole.
>
> Percent of whole is part.
> What percent of 48 is 30?

**Step 3:** Solve the proportion to find the percentage.

Cross multiply the terms you know.

$100 \times 30 = 3{,}000$

Divide by the term that is left, 48.

$3{,}000 \div 48 = 62.5$

The solved proportion is

$$\frac{62.5}{100} = \frac{30}{48}$$

**30 is 62.5% of 48.**

# Fractional Percents

*What percent of 3 is 1?*

**Step 1:** Set up a proportion.

$$\frac{\text{percentage}}{100} = \frac{\text{part}}{\text{whole}}$$

**Step 2:** Fill in what you know.

$$\frac{\text{percentage}}{100} = \frac{1}{3}$$

**Step 3:** Solve the proportion.
Cross multiply the terms you know, 100 and 1. Divide by the term that is left, 3.

$$3 \overline{)100} \;\; 33\tfrac{1}{3}$$

$$\begin{array}{r} -9 \\ \hline 10 \\ -9 \\ \hline 1 \end{array}$$

Write the remainder as $\frac{1}{3}$.

$100 \times 1 = 100$

$100 \div 3 = 33\tfrac{1}{3}$

$$\frac{33\tfrac{1}{3}}{100} = \frac{1}{3}$$

**1 is $33\tfrac{1}{3}$% of 3.**

# ㉒ Finding the Total

Sometimes you know
the percent and the part, and
you need to find the whole.

## Use a Proportion

*One serving of tomato soup
contains 1 gram of fiber.
This is 4% of the amount of
fiber recommended for one day.
How many grams of fiber are
recommended for one day?*

**Step 1:** Set up a proportion.

$$\frac{\text{percentage}}{100} = \frac{\text{part}}{\text{whole}}$$

**Step 2:** Fill in what you know.

$$\frac{4}{100} = \frac{1}{\text{whole}}$$

**Step 3:** Solve the proportion.
Cross multiply the terms you know, 100 and 1.    $100 \times 1 = 100$
Divide by the term that is left, 4.    $100 \div 4 = 25$

$$\frac{4}{100} = \frac{1}{25}$$

**25 grams of fiber are
recommended for one day.**

Proportion Buster:

Proportions can be used
to solve any percent problem.

You can find the part,
whole, or percent with a
proportion.

# The Percent Statement

*Complete this statement.*
*50% of ____ is 60.*

**Step 1:** Write the problem.
The problem is written using
the percent statement.
Change the statement to an equation.

50% of ____ is 60.
50% × ____ = 60

**Step 2:** Write the percent as a decimal.

0.50 × ____ = 60

**Step 3:** You can write a multiplication
with a missing factor as a division problem.
Divide the product by the factor you know.

60 ÷ 0.50 = ____

**Step 4:** Divide. When you divide by a
decimal, make the decimal a whole number
by moving the same number of places
in each number.

60.0 ÷ 0.50 = ____

600 ÷ 5 = ____
600 ÷ 5 = 120
so, 0.50 × 120 = 60

**50% of 120 is 60.**

*A serving of crackers contains 720 mg of sodium.*
*This is 30% of the sodium recommended for one day.*
*How many milligrams of sodium are recommended for one day?*

**Step 1:** Write the percent equation.
Put in the numbers you know.

percent × whole = part
30% × ____ = 720

**Step 2:** Write the percent as a decimal.  0.30 × ____ = 720

**Step 3:** Write the problem as division.

720 ÷ 0.30 = ____

**Step 4:** Divide.

720.0 ÷ 0.30 = ____

7,200 ÷ 3 = ____
7,200 ÷ 3 = 2,400
so, 0.30 × 2,400 = 720

**2,400 milligrams of sodium are recommended for one day.**

# 23 Percent of Change

This year, you have one more pet than you did last year. Is that a big change? It *is* if you only had one pet last year. It *is not* if you already had 20 pets. A percent of change compares an amount of change to the original amount.

## Percent of Increase

*A high school had 240 students last year. This year, there are 261 students at the same school. What is the percent of increase in the number of students?*

**Percent of increase** is the percent of change when an amount goes up.

**Step 1:** Subtract to find the change between the new number of students and the original number of students.

$$\text{new - original = change}$$
$$261 - 240 = 21$$

**Step 2:** Write a ratio of the change to the original.

$$\frac{\text{change}}{\text{original}} \qquad \frac{21}{240}$$

**Step 3:** Reduce the ratio to lowest terms.

$$\frac{21}{240} = \frac{7}{80}$$

**Step 4:** Write the ratio as a percent.
Multiply the ratio by 100.
Reduce.
Add the percent sign.

$$\frac{7}{80} \times 100 = \frac{7}{\underset{4}{80}} \times \frac{\overset{5}{100}}{1} = \frac{35}{4}$$

$$= 8\frac{3}{4}$$

**The percent of increase in the number of students is $8\frac{3}{4}$ %.**

$$\frac{21}{240} = 8\frac{3}{4}\%$$

50

# Percent of Decrease

*For the final football game of the year, the price of a cup of hot chocolate went down from $1.25 to $1.00. What was the percent of decrease?*

> Percent of **decrease** is the percent of change when an amount goes down.

**Step 1:** Subtract to find the change between the new price and the original price.

original - new = change
$1.25 - $1.00 = $0.25

**Step 2:** Write a ratio of the change to the original.

$$\frac{change}{original} \qquad \frac{0.25}{1.25}$$

**Step 3:** Write the ratio as a decimal by dividing the first term by the second term.

$$0.25 \div 1.25 = 0.2$$

$$1.25\overline{)0.250} \qquad 125\overline{)25.0}$$
$$\phantom{1.25)0.250} \qquad \underline{-\ 250}$$
$$\phantom{1.25)0.250} \qquad \qquad 0$$

**Step 4:** Write 0.2 as a percent. Move the decimal point 2 places right. Write the percent symbol.

0.2 = 20%

**The percent of decrease was 20%.**

# ㉔ Sales Tax and Discounts

When you buy an item
sometimes it costs you more than the
the marked price. Sales tax is money collected by
the government when you buy certain things.

## Sales Tax

*Marita spent the day at the mall. She bought a sweater with a price of $30.00. The sales tax was 7.5%. How much was the sales tax on the sweater?*

To solve this problem, find 7.5% of $30.00.

**Step 1:** Write the percent equation.  **percent × whole = part**
Put in the numbers you know.    **7.5%  × $30.00 = ___**

**Step 2:** Write the percent as a decimal.  **0.075 × $30.00 = ___**

**Step 3:** Multiply.    **0.075 × $30.00 = $2.25**

**7.5% of $30.00 is $2.25.**

## Total Cost

*What was the total cost of Marita's sweater from the problem above?*

**Step 1:** To find the total cost of an item, add the price and the sales tax.

price:        $30.00
sales tax:    + $  2.25
total cost:     $32.25

Sales tax percents are set by state and local governments.

Items with the same price may have a different total cost in different states or cities.

**The total cost of the sweater was $32.25.**

52

# What is a Discount?

A **discount** is an amount that is taken off the original price of an item. Some discounts are a dollar amount, like $2 off the price of a meal. Other discounts are a percent, like 10% off the price of an oil change.

## Discounts

*Every Monday, tropical fish at the pet store are discounted 25%. If the original price of a fish is $2.60, how much is the discount?*

To solve this problem, find 25% of $2.60.

**Step 1:** Write the percent equation. Put in the numbers you know.

**percent** × **whole** = **part**
25% × $2.60 = ____

**Step 2:** Write the percent as a decimal.

0.25 × $2.60 = ____

**Step 3:** Multiply.

0.25 × $2.60 = $0.65

**The discount on a fish that costs $2.60 is $0.65.**

## Sale Price

*What is the sale price of the fish from the problem above?*

**Step 1:** To find the sale price of an item, subtract the discount from the original price.

| | |
|---|---|
| original price: | $2.60 |
| discount: | - $0.65 |
| sale price: | $1.95 |

**The sale price of the fish is $1.95.**

# Commission and Income

Some jobs are paid
on commission. When a salesperson
receives a certain percent of sales,
the amount is called his or her commission.

## Sales Commission

*Jameson is a real estate agent. He earned a commission of $5,200 for the sale of a $130,000 house. What percent of the sale was his commission?*

**Step 1:** Write the ratio comparing commission (part) to sale price (whole).

$$\frac{\text{part}}{\text{whole}} \quad \frac{\$5,200}{\$130,000}$$

**Step 2:** Write the ratio as a decimal.

$$\frac{\$5,200}{\$130,000} = \$5,200 \div \$130,000 = 0.04$$

**Step 3:** Write the decimal, $\quad 0.04 = 4\%$ 0.04, as a percent.

**Jameson's commission was 4% of the sale.**

*Large even amounts of money, like $5,200 and $130,000 can be written without a decimal point. All of the zeros at the end can get confusing!*

## Use a Proportion

*At an appliance store, the salespeople earn a 12% commission when they sell an extended warranty. If the warranty costs $200.00, how much is the commission?*

**Step 1:** Set up a proportion.

$$\frac{\text{percentage}}{100} = \frac{\text{part}}{\text{whole}}$$

**Step 2:** Fill in what you know.

$$\frac{2}{100} = \frac{\text{part}}{\$200.00}$$

**Step 3:** Solve the proportion. Cross multiply the terms you know. Divide by the term that is left.

$$12 \times 200.00 = 2400.00$$
$$2400.00 \div 100 = 24.00$$

**The commission is $24.00.**

# Income

**gross income**—The total amount of income before taxes and other deductions are taken out.

**net income**—The amount that is left over after taxes and other deductions are taken out.

# Income

*Jameson earned $5,200 in commission. If 21% was taken out of his pay in deductions, how much was his net income?*

To solve this problem, first find the amount of deductions. Then subtract the deductions from $5,200.

**Step 1:** Find the amount of deductions by finding 21% of $5,200.

| | |
|---|---|
| Write the percent equation. | **percent × whole = part** |
| Put in the numbers you know. | **21% × $5,200 = _____** |

**Step 2:** Write the percent as a decimal.   **0.21 × $5,200 = _____**

**Step 3:** Multiply.                    **0.21 × $5,200 = $1,092**

**deductions = $1,092**

**Step 4:** Subtract the deductions, $1,092, from Jameson's gross pay, $5,200.

$$\begin{array}{r} \$5,200 \\ -\ \$1,092 \\ \hline \$4,108 \end{array}$$

**Jameson's net income was $4,108.**

# ㉖ Tips

Some jobs are paid by the hour.
Some are paid on commission. Part of the pay for other jobs is from the tips given by customers.

## What is a Tip?

People who provide a service are often given a **tip**.
Some service people are porters, waiters, and hairdressers.
Tips are usually given as a percent of the cost of the service.
For example, if a haircut costs $10.00, you might give the hairdresser a tip of 20%, or $2.00.

## Tips

*Cheyenne ate dinner at a restaurant. Her meal cost $17.89. She wants to give the waitress a tip that is close to 15%. About how much should she tip the waitress?*

**Step 1:** A tip is not usually a set amount, or a set percent. By rounding amounts to the nearest dollar, you can quickly decide how much to tip.

Round $17.89 to the nearest whole dollar.      Rounds to
$17.89 ⟶ $18.00

**Step 2:** Find 15% of $18.00.

$15\% \times \$18.00 = \_\_\_\_$
$0.15 \times \$18.00 = \$2.70$

**Cheyenne should tip about $2.70**

You could also round the tip amount to the nearest dollar. $2.70 rounds to $3.00.

## Multiplying by 10%

Look at 10% of some amounts. Do you see a pattern?

**10% of $70.00 is $7.00**          **10% of $7.00 is $0.70**

**10% of $42.00 is $4.20**          **10% of $4.20 is $0.42**

To find 10% of an amount, you can move the decimal point one place to the left.

## Mental Math

*A haircut costs $25.00. Use mental math to find the amount of a 20% tip on the haircut.*

**Step 1:** Think:          **I can find 10% of $25.00 by moving the decimal point one place left.**

**10% of $25.00 is $2.50**

**Step 2:** Think:          **20% is the same as 10% + 10%**

**20% = $2.50 + $2.50 = $5.00**

**A 20% tip on $25.00 is $5.00.**

# ㉗ Simple Interest

For some bank accounts,
like savings accounts, a bank will pay you
a set percent to borrow your money.

## Interest Terms

**principal**—The amount of money in an account.
**interest rate**—The percent that is paid by the borrower.
**simple interest**—Interest that is found one time on the principal.
To find simple interest multiply the principal, interest rate, and
time in years.

**Interest = Principal × Rate × Time, or**
**I = P × R × T**

## Simple Interest

*Find the simple interest on $300.00 for 2 years at 6%.*

| | |
|---|---|
| **Step 1:** Write the equation for simple interest. Fill in the amounts you know. | Interest = Principal × Rate × Time<br>Interest = $300.00 × 6% × 2 years |
| **Step 2:** Change the percent to a decimal. Write it in the equation. | 6% = 0.06<br>Interest = $300.00 × 0.06 × 2 |
| **Step 3:** Multiply. | Interest = ($300.00 × 0.06) × 2<br>= ($18.00) × 2<br>= $36.00<br><br>The simple interest is $36.00. |

# Time

Since interest is found using years, change all time values to years. For example, to change months to years, divide the number of months by the number of months in a year, 12.

These are some terms used for time when finding interest.
**annually**—One time a year.
**semiannually**—Every six months. $6 \div 12 = \frac{1}{2}$ or 0.5.
**quarterly**—Every three months. $3 \div 12 = \frac{1}{4}$ or 0.25.
**monthly**—Every month. $1 \div 12 = \frac{1}{12}$ or about 0.08.

# Semiannual Interest

*Find the semiannual interest on $1,000.00 at 8%.*

| | |
|---|---|
| **Step 1:** Write the equation for simple interest. Semiannual means every six months. Fill in the amounts you know. | **Interest = Principal × Rate × Time**<br>**Interest = $1,000.00 × 8% × 6 months** |
| **Step 2:** Change months to years. Write it in the equation. | **6 months = 0.5 years**<br>**Interest = $1,000.00 × 8% × 0.5** |
| **Step 3:** Change the percent to a decimal. Write it in the equation. | **8% = 0.08**<br>**Interest = $1,000.00 × 0.08 × 0.5** |
| **Step 4:** Multiply. | **Interest = ($1,000.00 × 0.08) × 0.5**<br>**= ($80.00) × 0.5**<br>**= $40.00** |

**The semiannual simple interest is $40.00.**

# ㉘ Compound Interest

Compound interest is interest
that is paid on principal *and* interest that has
already been earned.

## Compound Interest

*Find the compound interest on $300.00 for 2 years
at 6% compounded annually.*

**Step 1:** To find compound interest, find the simple interest for each period of time the amount is compounded. This account is compounded annually, or yearly, so find the simple interest for the first year.

| | |
|---|---|
| Write the equation for simple interest. Fill in the amounts you know. | **Interest = Principal × Rate × Time**<br>**Interest = $300.00 × 6% × 1 year** |

**Step 2:** Change the percent to a decimal. Write it in the equation.

$$6\% = 0.06$$
**Interest = $300.00 × 0.06 × 1**

**Step 3:** Multiply. This is the interest earned the first year.

**Interest = ($300.00 × 0.06) × 1**
**= ($18.00) × 1**
**= $18.00**

**Step 4:** Add the principal and the interest from the first year. This is the new principal.

| | |
|---|---|
| **principal** | $300.00 |
| **interest** | + $  18.00 |
| **new principal** | $318.00 |

**Step 5:** Find the interest earned the second year using the new principal.

| | |
|---|---|
| Write the equation for simple interest. Fill in the amounts you know. | **Interest = Principal × Rate × Time**<br>**Interest = $318.00 × 6% × 1 year** |

**Step 6:** Change the percent to a decimal. Write it in the equation.

$$6\% = 0.06$$
**Interest = $318.00 × 0.06 × 1**

**Step 7:** Multiply. This is the interest earned the second year.

Interest = ($318.00 × 0.06) × 1
= ($19.08) × 1
= $19.08

**Step 8:** The question asked for the compound interest over 2 years.

| | |
|---|---|
| **first year** | $ 18.00 |
| **second year** | + $ 19.08 |
| | $ 37.08 |

The compound interest is $37.08.

## Compounding

*If you save money in an account that compounds quarterly for 3 years, how many times will it compound?*

**Step 1:** Multiply the number of times the money compounds each year by the number of years the money is saved.

Compound interest earns more money than simple interest when the interest rate and time are the same.

On page 58, using simple interest, the same savings account earned $36.

When an account compounds quarterly, it compounds 4 times every year.

**4 times a year × 3 years = 12 times**

**The money will compound 12 times.**

Some accounts compound daily. That's 365 times every year!

Calculator, anyone?

# Further Reading

## Books

Enzensberger, Hans Magnus. *The Number Devil: A Mathematical Adventure.* New York: Owl Books, 2000.

Great Source Education Group, Inc. *Math On Call.* Wilmington, Mass.: Great Source Education Group, Inc., 2004.

School Specialty Publishing. *The Complete Book of Math.* Grand Rapids, Mich.: School Specialty Publishing, 2001.

## Internet Addresses

Math.com. "Pre-Algebra." © 2000–2007.
<http://www.math.com/homeworkhelp/PreAlgebra.html>

The Math Forum. "Ask Dr. Math." © 1994–2007.
<http://mathforum.org/library/drmath/sets/elem_golden.html>
<http://mathforum.org/library/drmath/sets/mid_fractions.html>

Spector, Lawrence. *The Math Page.* "Skill in Arithmetic." © 2001–2007.
<http://www.themathpage.com/ARITH/arithmetic.htm>

# Index